A Daughter's Keeper

Crystal Antoinette Johnson

A Daughter's Keeper

Crystal Antoinette Johnson

Printed in the United States of America
First Printing, 2021

ISBN 978-1-7359807-5-1

 Publisher: Brittney Holmes Jackson & Co.
Stonecrest, GA 30038
www.BrittneyHolmesJackson.com

To the Lost Girls.

Your Father is calling you home.

Acknowledgements

ABBA Father, I will never have words adequate enough to express what You mean to me. Thank You for leaving the 99 for this hardheaded 1. I appreciate this journey of finding You, which turned into finding myself. Thank You for Your unconditional love, forgiveness, and unmerited favor. As Your favoritest girl in the world, I hope to make You proud and bring a smile to Your face. I thank You for the crown of beauty You gave me for my ashes, for the boldness to come out of the shadows, and for love that washed me that I may shine like a star. Love always!

To my dad Elliot Johnson, we couldn't have ever known what our journey would bring. As a maturing daughter, I recognize it all was necessary. Our relationship has truly taught me the meaning of love from the definition of 1 Corinthians 13:4-7. I appreciate all that you have done for me and all that you continue to do. I am thankful that you are my dad and I hope that I make you proud -Your first born.

To my mom, I can only pray to make you proud. You have been my rock through many of life's transitions. You have seen the best and worst of me and always supported in love. I know that your prayers are a part of the reason I am still here. Thank you for never giving up on me. For your patience, love, and support.

To my sonshine, Rinji. I know you probably won't read this book because it's for girls but you are a huge part of my story. I am so blessed to have such a wonderful son. It is often in my moments of parenting you that God parents me! Know that God loves His sons too and He has a great future and destiny in store for you. I pray that all the moments of worship, prayer, and biblical discussions in your youth will be a seed that harvests in your future. Remember, God is your all in one.

To my sisters: J5, we have been through the trenches! With similar yet different experiences, I pray that God would continue to heal and redeem your stories. I pray that my growing relationship with God encourages you to continue to pursue Him past any fears or limitations life tries to put on you. Far more awaits you.

Table of Contents

Foreword

It is a privilege to write the foreword for this work by Crystal. She is my eldest child and is the most vivid image of the "rose that grew from concrete." She is a strong woman of character, and I am very proud of her.

One of the things that I tried to instill in Crystal was the concept of identity. This attempt was inadequate because of shortcomings on my end as her father. Her grandparents on my side of the family grew up in Jim Crow New Orleans, Louisiana. They experienced racism and discrimination to a level that neither Crystal nor I would ever face. However, they were given the grace to attend Dillard University in New Orleans and would later attend graduate school and become middle class professionals. Much of their identity came from the civil rights movement and the African American church.

I was raised with the same kind of identity paradigm. Unfortunately, it was difficult for me to feel secure when my sense of identity was based on the struggle for civil rights and the sad fact that my ancestors were slaves. This insecurity continued as I went off to a predominately white undergraduate institution and interacted with students who could trace their ancestry to specific locations in the United Kingdom or Europe. These students had great pride in their ancestry and bloodline, and it grounded them. It was different for me, because my side of the family could only trace its ancestry back to the San Francisco Plantation in Garyville, Louisiana. When one's identity is connected to slavery, one's outlook on the world can become clouded. It has always been difficult for me to really know who I am for that reason, I have sought proxies for identity all of my life just so that I could feel "normal."

Even in church, my concept and understanding of Christianity was based on the struggle for civil rights. Unfortunately, I did not receive teaching about identity in Christ.

This work that Crystal has developed is very important in

enlightening the disconnected and the disenfranchised of all racial backgrounds. While it is important to know one's ancestry, it is more important to be able to trace one's bloodline back to the Lord Jesus Christ. After all, that is why He came in person to the planet. The human bloodline originally traced back to the Creator. However, due to the sin of Adam and Eve in the Garden of Eden, that bloodline was altered and connected by their choices to the kingdom of darkness. All humans that are born on the Earth are automatically linked by blood to the king of darkness. In order to give humans the chance to restore their bloodline to the true and living God, Jesus was sent to suffer, bleed, and die for our sins, so that we could once again have the opportunity to be called the sons and daughters of the Most High God. Christianity is all about bloodline.

In this book, Crystal expands upon identity through Christ Jesus and how it saves, heals, delivers, and provides peace.

by Elliot Stanley Johnson

I was the sum of everything
that happened to me
and yet could not see why I kept
falling.
Petals in the wind,
A puppet of their imagination,
I morphed into whatever their
heart was longing.
Both hungry and thirsty I ran to
and fro
But nothing ever satisfied this
yearning.
Until I ripped off the veil,
And looked into the glass:
I was a caged bird in mourning.

Fly free.

A DAUGHTER'S KEEPER

Identity

"Know, first, who you are, and then adorn yourself accordingly." – Epictetus

Who are you?

Since the fall of man, we have been searching to find ourselves. Who we are is often built on the words, expectations, and experiences we have with others. We pride ourselves on the titles and accolades we receive, and they become the pillars of who we are. So, when the storms of life come and shake these accessories, we call identity, we end up with moments of identity crisis. Mother, sister, wife, daughter, teacher, nurse, judge, etc. Right? It's so easy to talk about what we do. But that's not who we are. These positions or relationships are life experiences in which we express our true selves.

> **Identity:** the fact of being who or what a person or thing is. *(Oxford Languages)*

Before you can improve any relationship, you must go back to the foundation. And that is understanding truly who you are.

Let me reassure you of what you are not! You are not your title, position, or your past. You are not your mistakes or moments of heartbreak. You are a Child of God. And now it's time to understand that, own it, and walk in it!

> *"Your identity is not about who you are in appearance, or power, or abilities, or status, it's simply about God setting His love on you and making you a part of His family."–*
> *Glenn C. Stewart*

We must shift from seeing ourselves based on the things we have done and the experiences that were forced upon us. Every day we must renew our mind with the Word of God which is infallible. In this chapter, soak in these truths which are founded in the Word of God.

We must shift from seeing ourselves based on the things we have done and the experiences that were forced upon us. Every day we must renew our mind with the Word of God which is infallible. In this chapter, soak in these truths which are founded in the Word of God.

You are loved and wanted.

The sacrifice of His son on your behalf is proof that you are loved. God who is holy wanted to make sure there was a way for us to have an eternal relationship with Him and reside in Heaven with Him, so out of love, Jesus died for our sins.

> *"What do you think? If a man owns a hundred sheep, and one of them wanders away, will he not leave the ninety-nine on the hills and go to look for the one that wandered off? And if he finds it, truly I tell you, he is happier about that one sheep than about the ninety-nine that did not wander off. In the same way your Father in heaven is not willing that any of these little ones should perish."*
> *– Matthew 18:12-14 NIV*

His love for you is not based on merit or accolades. It is not based on if you had a perfect day. It. Just. Is. And because of this great love, He pursues us with open arms, even on our worst days. Take heart, Daughter of God, the Almighty One promises to love you until the end of time. And His word never returns unto Him void.

You were chosen and made in His image.

> *"So God created mankind in His own image, in the image of God he created them; male and female He created them."*
> *– Genesis 1:27 NIV*

It is so important that your identity be built on a solid foundation. A truth that is not conditional, no matter the circumstance. And the truth is God chose to make us as He crafted the world. And He used Himself as the blueprint.

I'm sure that you have heard the following before:
"You're just like your mother…"
"You get that from your father…"
"That's just how our family handles things…"

It is hard to walk in the absolute freedom of who God has called us to be when life and people tell us who we are from the moment we are born. They heap clichés and declarations on us based on our families and their perception. And over time, we begin to believe them too. The problem with this thinking is that it places you in a box. Who you are or become is bound by the characteristics of your family and the storyline your life has ventured through to that point? This will always cause us to hit the glass ceiling when God is calling us to fly.

> *"But you are a chosen generation, a royal priesthood, a holy nation, His own special people, that you may proclaim the praises of Him who called you out of darkness into His marvelous light."*
> *– 1 Peter 2:9 NKJV*

Daughters of God, *you were chosen.* You are no mistake, no accident. No matter the circumstances around your birth, God deliberately made a way for your arrival on earth at that particular time and on that particular date. You were handcrafted by the Creator of the world and He calls you daughter. You are royalty because He is King. He chose not only to make you, but to love you, and walk alongside you every day. And because we are made in His image, there will never be a ceiling to your evolution because we will never reach perfection this side of Heaven.

You are a new creation

> *Your true identity starts when you accept Christ as your Lord and Savior. "Therefore, if anyone is in Christ, he is a new creation. The old has passed away; behold, the new has come."*
> *– 2 Corinthians 5:17 NIV*

New life is your portion. No matter what life has looked like, there is newness in Christ. You are no longer bound to the ways of this world. Instead, you are able to journey with the Creator to become who He created you to be.

Sweet Sister, I know that you have made mistakes. I have too … Plenty of them. But our gracious Lord remembers them no more when we confess our sins and repent. Embrace newness of life. It is a gift from the One who sacrificed everything for you. Don't waste it by holding yourself hostage to your past.

You were made with a purpose on purpose.

Not only did God divinely create you on purpose. He created you *with purpose*. He picked the time period, the country, and the parents to conceive you. All of this was on purpose. He knew which of their talents, abilities, and personality traits you would inherit from them. He knew the impact and influence your city or town would have on you.

> *"For we are God's handiwork, created in Christ Jesus to do good works, which God prepared in advance for us to do."*
> *– Ephesians 2:10 NIV*

These nuances do not seem significant to us and quite frankly, sometimes they probably seem to be a detriment, but God looks at things from a different perspective. A heavenly perspective with a holistic view. Remember, when it comes to a kingdom, the King must place trusted people all over to make sure land is governed the right way.

You are an heir.

We come into this world only knowing our parents. And that relationship becomes the groundwork for our identity. But there is a lineage that trumps even that of our blood; the lineage of God through Jesus Christ.

IDENTITY

"Now if we are children, then we are heirs - heirs of God and co-heirs with Christ, if indeed we share in his sufferings in order that we may also share in his glory."
— Romans 8:17 NIV

When we accept Jesus Christ as our Lord and Savior, there is a shift in the blood. The sacrifice of Jesus Christ covers us and we become a new creation. At that point, we are no longer orphans, servants, or slaves, but children of the Most High. And because he is a King that makes us heirs in the kingdom of heaven.

"If you don't know where you've come from, you don't know where you're going." — Maya Angelou

It's important to grasp this fact because it shows who you are and what has been given to you. If you don't know who you come from, then you won't be able to operate in the authority and dominion given to you. Your perspective on life will be limited as will be the reach of your influence.

"Very truly I tell you, whoever believes in me will do the works I have been doing, and they will do even greater things than these, because I am going to the Father. And I will do whatever you ask in my name, so that the Father may be glorified in the Son. You may ask me for anything in my name, and I will do it."
— John 14:12-14 NIV

God is sovereign, righteous, and holy. He is perfect, He is powerful, and He is eternal. He is proclaimed as the King of Kings and Lord of Lords and because you have been adopted into His family, you have a new title and rank: Queen! And even better than recognizing God as King is that He looks at you and loves you as a Father.

You are a Daughter!

This great and mighty God is not just sitting in the heavens watching us from "on high". He is very active and very present in our lives. God is relational! And He desires to have a close relationship with you. Once you accept Him as Father, you become His beloved daughter.

"But to all who did receive him, who believed in his name, he gave the right to become children of God."
— John 1:12 ESV

My prayer for you is that through this book, you will find the courage to shake off the shackles that have held you bound and fly free in the identity that is true. You are a daughter of God. You are in the lineage of Christ - beautifully and wonderfully made.

Becoming all you are meant to be starts with a relationship with God. So often we look at Him as this benevolent far away being. This God who sits way up high and looks down low. But He's not just God, He is our Father.

Prayer

Father God,

Thank You for everlasting love. For Your patience and grace. Thank You for choosing me Lord, in spite of myself. Lord, that You love me enough to allow me to be a part of Your family and a willing participant in Your legacy. I'm so glad that You do not see Your children through earthly eyes but through heaven's gaze. I am overwhelmed by a love that would allow me to stand in Your presence though I am not worthy. Help me to see me as You do. Help me to love me as You do. Help me to truly understand who I am in You. To walk in the identity of Your Daughter. As I learn my identity in You, I pray that everything else falls into place. Guide me Father, that I may produce lasting fruit that is pleasing in Your sight.

In Jesus' name,
Amen.

Love Moment

Write a list of 10 attributes that speak to who you are. None of these attributes can be a job or relationship like doctor, mother, friend, teacher, etc. Some good examples are beautiful, accepted, loved, and creative.

_____
_____
_____
_____
_____
_____
_____
_____
_____
_____
_____
_____
_____
_____
_____
_____
_____
_____
_____
_____
_____
_____

ABBA

"I have loved you with an everlasting love; I have drawn you with unfailing kindness. I will build you up again."
– Jeremiah 31:3-4 NIV

Hi, my name is Crystal and I used to be a bonafide daddy's girl.

Daddy's Girl: *A girl (adult or child) who has a strong bond with her father, typically the bond to her father is stronger than the bond to her mother, the term may sometimes infer that she's been spoiled as a child. – Urban Dictionary*

I am the oldest of six girls, but my dad was my best friend. I used to read the same types of books he read, watched him play Warcraft on the computer, and watched Star Trek with him all day. I was proud. And I tried to always bring honor to my family by getting good grades and excelling. And once I started attending the high school that he worked at....well, you couldn't tell me nothing! Despite the negative moments I experienced, I wanted to be close to him. I wanted to make him proud and to be the one who put a smile on his face. And so, my world crashed when my parents divorced, and he left us. I was 17.

> **Law of Similarity**: *a Gestalt principle of organization holding that (other things being equal) parts of a stimulus field that are similar to each other tend to be perceived as belonging together as a unit.*

While the concept of God may be easy for many of us to grasp, I believe the concept of Father is not. Many of us have less than fairytale stories about our earthly fathers. We have scars and some open wounds that we try to ignore as we survive. But what we did not/do not know is how that earthly connection has so much influence on our heavenly one. Unknowingly, we limit the presence of God in our lives because we look at Him through the lens of fallible men. Through the lens of mistrust, distrust, rejection, and abuse.

But God is not fallible.

God is not your (earthly) father.

> **Father:** *to be the founder, producer, or author of*
> *c: to accept responsibility for*
> *to fix the paternity or origin of*
> *: to care for or look after someone as a father might*

> **Fatherhood:** *A male parent; one who loves, supports, guides, inspires,*
> *and encourages his children. A man of strong character who teaches by example.*

A good father's role in your life will have four major functions: to protect, correct, guide, and love.

Protects:

Whether we realize it or not, we are recipients of heavenly protection. That car accident that could have been worse, the guy who lost interest, the opportunity that fell through our hands. These were all moments when God's divine hand was at work in our lives. Now some of these things you may not consider protection. If we were honest, some of these things were things we desired. But a good father, in all of his wisdom and experience, can see a potential threat and moves to neutralize it. Our Father God knows the thoughts of every person and what is taking place behind the scenes. And because He loves us, He protects us from it.

> *He will guard and guide me, never letting me stumble or fall. God is my keeper; he will never forget nor ignore me. He will never slumber nor sleep; he is the Guardian - God for his people, Israel. Jehovah himself will watch over you; He's always at your side to shelter you safely in His presence. He's protecting you from all danger both day and night. He will keep you from every form of evil or calamity as He continually watches over you. You will be guarded by God Himself. You will be safe when you leave your home and safely you will return. He will protect you now, and He'll protect you forevermore! – Psalm 121:3-8 TPT*

Like a shepherd to sheep so does a father to his children. We must learn that sometimes a closed door, a failed relationship, or even leaving the house late are forms of divine protection. Remember, God wants the best for us and so anything that will bring us unnecessary pain or anguish He will move to protect us from.

And that brings us to God's rules. God gives us the freedom to choose the decisions we make and the type of life we want to live. But as a good Father, He set up rules and standards for living to help us along the way.

Corrects:

When I was in middle school, I began to get more chores. Cleaning the bathroom (hated it) and washing the dishes. As any preteen would, sometimes I didn't do my best. I would clean half of the dinner dishes and leave the rest until the next day.

One day, my dad was tired of my shenanigans. He woke me up at 1am and sent me upstairs alone to finish the dishes. In this house, the bedrooms were in the basement and the living room, kitchen, and computer room were upstairs. I was scared out of my skin!!! Man, I finished those dishes as fast as I could, shut the door, and ran back downstairs to my room. As much as I hated it at the time, my dad was teaching me a valuable lesson. There are consequences for disobedience. How important it is to do things right the first time. He was setting a standard for the quality of work I produced. Lastly, he was preparing me for adult life so that I could take care of myself and in turn, teach my son the same principles. So on days when I don't feel like working, I push through. The cleanliness of my home is due to years of cultivating good maintenance habits. What seemed like a waste of time because it was "just dishes" became a cornerstone in my character that I will need for the rest of my life.

The fact of the matter is no one likes to be disciplined. No matter how big or small, we pout, roll our eyes, and stubbornly refuse to glean anything from those tough parental moments. But ultimately, those are the moments that help shape us into the people we were meant to be. Those are the moments that instill humility, respect, and keep us on the right path. As our Heavenly Father, God does the same thing.

> *My son, do not despise the Lord's discipline or be weary of his reproof, for the Lord reproves him whom he loves, as a father the son in whom he delights.* – Proverbs 3:11-12 ESV

Lessons are often served as humble pie.

When my last relationship ended in 2019, I was very angry. I cut it completely off, deleted his number, blocked him on all social media. I began to ask God to help me and cut the soul tie between us. I was serious about preparing for my future husband and I no longer wanted any parts of relationship games. There was absolutely no communication between us. I would talk about him here and there, vent, even into 2020. Although I wasn't as angry, I still had questions on why he had ghosted me and was talking to someone else while he was talking to me. Although I had no desire to talk to him, it seemed like I couldn't fully let it go.

In June 2020, I attended a three-day conference called the Identity and Purpose Summit with Dr. Faith Wokoma. After the last live session was over, God spoke to me. *"Email him and apologize."* Apologize?!?! "Lord, what am I apologizing for? I didn't do anything!" I was not having it. I could feel God urging me to apologize but I was proud. He messed up not me, and you want me to say sorry??? Nah, bruh.

Transparent moment: I'm super hardheaded, y'all. It legit took me a week to submit to God. I promise you He was tugging on me every day, but I wasn't having it. At 11:35pm on July 3rd, I sent this message:

> *I apologize for handling my frustrations and emotions wrong. While I may not have vented to the entire world, the people that I did vent to know you as well. I did not take into account your feelings or even how it may have affected your dealings or relationships with others. The Word says love covers and, in those moments, I did not exhibit godly love for you. For that I apologize.*

Whew.

The humble pie was having to recognize I was still responsible for my actions regardless of what someone else did. A broken heart is not a license to act a fool, operate in bitterness or unforgiveness. God was showing me that He held me responsible for my stewardship of my Brother in Christ too. And I couldn't fully move on or be free until I apologized and repented of my sin. That correction hurt and my pride was wounded, but God was right. It gave me a fresh perspective on all my relationships: family, friends, and lover. We have a responsibility to God for how we care for the people He places in our lives. And if we leave them worse instead of better, that part is on us too. My ex responded a couple days later, and a weight lifted off of me. I received the closure I wasn't even looking for, and I was able to truly put that situation behind me and move forward.

A good father who loves you will do what it takes to help you become a better person who makes wise decisions. That means confronting the lies, holding us to a higher standard, and chastising us when we are wrong. Think about your childhood. Most people do not grow up and thank their parents for allowing them to do whatever they wanted. Most thank their parents for setting boundaries in place, for not giving up on them, for their patience, and support. Typically, as adults, we look back on those memories and see the critical moments that shaped the responsible, giving, dependable people we are today.

All those I dearly love I unmask and train. So repent and be eager to pursue what is right. – Revelation 3:19 TPT

Guides:
"For I know the plans I have for you," declares the Lord, "plans to prosper you and not to harm you, plans to give you hope and a future." – Jeremiah 29:11 NIV

A good father will not just see where you are currently, but everything you can become. For God, it's not a possibility but a guarantee! In His goodness, He will remove or add people and opportunities to our lives to help us continue towards the purpose that He has placed on the inside of each of us.

Our Heavenly Father desires such a relationship with you that He can be your all-in-one love. And He's great enough to pursue us for it! For me, He came on a day where I was longing for more and open enough to listen.

In April 2016, I went to the *It's Time* Women's Conference. This was my mom's first major speaking engagement, and I was her roll dog. On the last night of the conference there was an altar call, and I went up for prayer. As this woman prayed for me, she whispered: "You have to let that relationship die with your father. You must let it go. At least for right now." My heart broke in half. I was overcome with grief. To let go of the one thing, one person I was trying so hard to hold on to. But God wasn't being cruel. In order for me to see ABBA in a different way, He needed space in my life to be the supreme

Father figure. Because the enemy will use strife, rejection, and our humanity to keep us from truly being in a relationship with God. And as much as it hurt, I surrendered that relationship, and my life is all the better for it.

The goodness of God is He can cause that which is dead to live. That space of silence, of distance, of forgiveness; God created something new. And it came during one of my greatest challenges to date, which was leaving that 10-year relationship and starting life again as a single mom in 2017. The dissolution of combined finances and a two-parent household. Learning to live on my own for the very first time and I was losing my best friend. What girl doesn't need a dad at that point?!?! My entire world was falling apart, and I felt alone, lost at sea. My dad knew about it and also knew me. He understood my tendency to retreat and isolate. So, he called and checked on me. Sometimes it was only for two minutes, sometimes it was ten minutes. But he consistently began to reach out periodically. If he didn't hear from me in about a month, he was calling again. Although it was a lot to process, by God's grace, I journeyed forward with two fathers as my anchors. My father and I were able to move forward and forge what would become a new normal. A new father and daughter relationship.

Here I am in 2020, with a stronger sense of identity and a reserve of faith and perseverance. I would have never thought I would be here with the relationships I have now with both my heavenly and earthly fathers back in 2016. That He would use another broken relationship to be fertile ground for this one to grow. That in the days of my greatest need, my perspective of my dad would shift. He became present, committed, protective, and a source of wisdom and edification. God really does make all things work for our good.

God makes no errors.
God is not the sum of your father's failures.
He is consistent and unwavering.
His love is perfect.
Let that sink in.

Loves:

> *For I am persuaded that neither death nor life, nor angels nor*
> *principalities nor powers, nor things present nor things to come,*
> *nor height nor depth, nor any other created thing, shall be able to*
> *separate us from the love of God which is in Christ Jesus our*
> *Lord. – Romans 8:38-39 NKJV*

You are so loved by the Almighty. You were chosen and deemed royalty. You are His workmanship, handcrafted - an original earthly display of His heavenly being…He called you beautiful…Created to live in eternity with Him. Singing songs and loving Him…Basking in His presence, loved by Him. Father-daughter time for forever!

But He doesn't want to wait until you reach heaven, no He desires every day to have a relationship with you. God is able to handle your fears, your mistakes, your insecurities … None of your yuck scares Him! Instead, gently, He beckons into His presence. Many times, we disregard the call because of how we see ourselves. Because we fear rejection, we fear being vulnerable, because if we aren't performing well, will He still love us? But God is not looking for perfection. He doesn't care about the titles and accolades. He just wants the most precious part of you. Your heart.

There is no greater love than the One who sacrificed everything for you - that's something no human can do. This Holy God chose to come down from on high and meet you in your journey. In His Holiness, He meets us in our yuck and cleans us up. That's how good a Father He is! He lovingly disciplines and sews up our wounds. Our King Jesus is madly in love with you and NOTHING you do will make this untrue…

So set your eyes above the taunts of the enemy who seeks to prey on your insecurities and wounds of rejection. Don't fall into the traps he sets, meditating on the endless thoughts of "who will love me? Where's my daddy?" He's right here with you … They call Him

ABBA

Immanuel (God with us), the Comforter, and King. And you, sweet sister, are a part of His lineage - Queen.

Choose today to be brave. Open your heart to your Abba Father. He is everything you need, and He lovingly waits for you.

The Lord has appeared of old to me, saying: "Yes, I have loved you with an everlasting love; Therefore, with lovingkindness I have drawn you." – Jeremiah 31:3 NKJV

Prayer

Lord God,

I am in need of a father. I am grateful that despite my disappointments and fears, You are willing and able to be the Father that I need. Help me Lord, to surrender my hurt and broken heartedness to You. Help me to have the courage to open my heart to You so that I may embark on this Father-Daughter journey with You. Help me to see You like never before and learn to love You as my ABBA.

In Jesus' name, Amen.

And Lord,

I pray for my earthly father. I pray that he becomes the man of God you created him to be. Lord, I forgive him. I forgive him for the moments he could not be what I needed. I forgive him for the moments when I felt most rejected. I forgive him for abandoning me. Lord, I learn relationship with You, heal my relationship with him. As I learn what real love is, help me to love him too. Instill in me an air of compassion for him, understanding that he is just trying to figure out life too. He needs mercy, grace, and forgiveness just like I do. As You do a new work in me, I pray for restoration and healing in our relationship. Thank You for the testimony of love and wholeness that will glorify Your name.

In Jesus' name, Amen.

Love Moment

Write down 10 things you need from God as a Father.
(Do not try to rationalize what He can't do but just
honestly state what you need).

_____
_____
_____
_____
_____
_____
_____
_____
_____
_____
_____
_____
_____
_____
_____
_____
_____
_____
_____
_____
_____
_____
_____
_____

Thanks be to God,
Who goes after the one.
Who openly welcomes the Prodigal
son.
Who cleans our wounds,
And erases our shame.
Because of Your love,
We will never be the same.
Great are You Lord,
And worthy to be praised.
I will sing of Your loving kindness
For the rest of my days.

Real Love

*"Though the mountains be shaken, and the hills be removed, yet
my unfailing love for you will not be shaken nor my covenant of
peace be removed," says the Lord, who has compassion on you.*
– Isaiah 54:10 NIV

Love. Probably the most desired thing in the entire world.
Even more than money. How many movies do we watch with hope;
will the guy get the girl in the end? Will the Father rescue his daughter?
Everywhere we turn, there is an influence of love as we understand it.

Boy Meets World was one of my first influences. Airing in 1993,
at the age of seven I watched Cory fall in love with Topanga in middle
school. In high school, the two become a couple and later get married
in college. Who wouldn't want the boy next door story? Of high school
sweethearts?

Later in 2002, my junior year of high school, I found my
favorite movie to date: Brown Sugar. It's a story of two kids who were
best friends from a young age to 15 years later. They recognize
through other relationships, that they love and desire to be together.
The way they supported each other and the openness of their
friendship, y'all I just melted. I have always been in love with love. But
this kind of love - the love that society shows us - is false and super
dysfunctional. Love has become an overly misused word. In our
attempts to give love and receive love, it has become a myth. A rarely
seen shooting star. You know it exists but so few can attest to
experiencing such a wonder. Or what they claim to have is an
imposter.

Daughters of God, true love is real. And what we require in
terms of love isn't wrong or too much! Where we go wrong is the
source in which we seek the supply of love and devotion from. God
wants to show us true fatherhood and clear the illusions of what love
is. It is not a fairy tale. The truth is love has been present with you
before you were even born and has watched over you daily. Love

opens your eyes each morning and gives you the strength to face each day.

And that is God.

> *"...for love comes from God. Everyone who loves has been born of God and knows God. Whoever does not love does not know God, because God is love. This is how God showed His love among us: He sent His one and only Son into the world that we might live through Him. This is love: not that we loved God, but that He loved us and sent His Son as an atoning sacrifice for our sins.*
> *– 1 John 4:7-10 NIV*

In order to know and experience real love, we must go back to the originator of love. It is only in experiencing His perfect love first that we can identify what real love looks like in human form and also give it in return.

> **Love:** *is patient, love is kind. It does not envy, it does not boast, it is not proud. It does not dishonor others, it is not self-seeking, it is not easily angered, it keeps no record of wrongs. Love does not delight in evil but rejoices with the truth. It always protects, always trusts, always hopes, always perseveres.*
> *– 1 Corinthians 13:4-7 NIV*

How I met Love

One of the things I did in my newfound singleness was study the queens in the Bible. As I was reading the book of Esther, I was reminded of her year of preparation. She spent an entire year getting prepared to be presented before the king. I decided that I would do the same with a twist. I would take a year, not to prepare for a man but to grow in love with God. I purposed in my heart that for the next year, my heart was off limits to any man, period! Doing this would give me time to grow in love and allow God the space to heal what was broken within me. I'm not going to lie y'all, it was a bittersweet year to say the least. To heal, God had to uncover. There were many nights of tears, but they always ended with peace and waking each morning feeling a little bit lighter.

> *With my whole heart, with my whole life, and with my innermost being, I bow in wonder and love before you, the holy God! Yahweh, You are my soul's celebration. How could I ever forget the miracles of kindness You've done for me? You kissed my heart with forgiveness, in spite of all I've done. You've healed me inside and out from every disease. You've rescued me from hell and saved my life. You've crowned me with love and mercy. That's the goodness of God's love!* – Psalm 103: 1-4 TPT

Our Father God is beyond wonderful. He gives you the strength to confront your pains, disappointments, and mistakes, and covers it with love! He heals the parts of you that are hurting and broken. He shows you how you perceive yourself versus how He views you - the apple of His eye.

Now love is meant to be reciprocated. It's never just one way, God requires something of us in return:

> *Jesus replied: 'Love the Lord your God with all your heart and with all your soul and with all your mind.' This is the first and greatest commandment. And the second is like it: 'Love your neighbor as yourself.'* – Matthew 22:37-38

How to love the Sovereign One

How do you love someone you can't see? I get it, I had that question as well. God is still a parent and so to love Him is to honor Him the same way we do our parents. Outside of the physical moments of spending time and reverencing Him are two major ways to show God your love.

Time:

> *"Now, Israel, what does the Lord your God require from you, but to fear the Lord your God, to walk in all His ways and love Him, and to serve the Lord your God with all your heart and with all your soul."* – Deuteronomy 10:12

Spending time through prayer, worship, and devotion (reading the Word). Believe it or not, God cares very much about your devotion! Exodus 34:14 talks about His desire for our worship; "for you shall worship no other god, for the Lord, whose name is Jealous, is a jealous God."

Being obedient to His statutes and living righteously:

If you love me, keep My Commandments. – John 14:15 NKJV

Just like any relationship, your relationship with your Heavenly Father will bloom and grow. Just make sure your motives and heart are in the right place, and that is the position of love.

Self-love

Being patient with yourself. We can truly be our worst critic sometimes. The things we are compassionate about with others, we crucify ourselves for. We must learn to extend grace and mercy to ourselves. We are not perfect and have a lot to learn and unlearn. And because of His unconditional love and mercy, we don't have to walk the journey alone.

Self-care: What you care about, you will care for. We will spend money, buy gifts, and bend over backwards for our loved ones and friends. But when it comes to ourselves, we do not give ourselves half of the same energy.

I know for me, I became my last priority when I became a mom. In the more recent years, I am learning to slow down and have regular me time. I'm learning to not fill every space with a task. I'm learning it's ok to take a break. The more I take care of myself, the more capacity I have to take care of other people. No more running on E, ladies!

Yet you, Lord, are our Father. We are the clay, you are the potter; we are all the work of your hand. – Isaiah 64:8 NIV

Sweet sisters, we must learn to appreciate who God made us to be: stop being so critical! It is so easy for us as women to point out the things that we do not like about ourselves. Our wish list is a mile long. It's easy to fantasize about all the cosmetic changes we would make if we had the money. "I wish I could change my weight; I wish I could change my complexion. Oh, if I had a bigger butt, I would love to add a cup size or two …" We compare ourselves to the celebrities and IG models and feel inferior. And even when we do receive a compliment, we often follow it up with a criticism of ourselves. But the Word of God says we are fearfully and wonderfully made.

You are altogether beautiful, my darling; there is no flaw in you.
– Song of Songs 4:7 NIV

Empathy, Mercy, & an aunt called, Grace

Sometimes it's hard to see people beyond what they do to us - good or bad. Many of the traumas or sour moments we experience are due to some form of interaction with people. It's so easy to turn up our noses and judge their story. To say what they should have done or what you would have done in their position. But let someone come for our stories … It's time to fight! A part of love is granting grace and mercy to others even when they don't deserve it. It is having compassion as people struggle in their own journeys.

When he saw the vast crowds of people, Jesus' heart was deeply moved with compassion, because they seemed weary and helpless, like wandering sheep without a shepherd. – Matthew 9:36 TPT

Empathy: *the ability to recognize, understand, and share the thoughts and feelings of another person, animal, or fictional character. Developing empathy is crucial for establishing relationships and behaving compassionately.*
– Psychology Today

We must remember, they are lost just like we once were. And when they find Jesus, that's when their journey begins. And everyone is facing a battle as they climb the hill of life. God was/ is patient with us and gave us grace and mercy as we matured in Him. And even as far as we have come, there is still more refining that we must go through. That love, grace, patience, and mercy isn't for a select group, it's for anyone who believes in Him and is willing to do the work. We must learn that people are not our enemies, but rather lost brothers and sisters is Christ, looking for THE answer. And we, having been reacquainted with our Father, can offer them hope and love while showing them the way.

> *Therefore encourage one another and build one another up, just as you are doing. We ask you, brothers, to respect those who labor among you and are over you in the Lord and admonish you, and to esteem them very highly in love because of their work. Be at peace among yourselves. And we urge you, brothers, admonish the idle, encourage the fainthearted, help the weak, be patient with them all.*
> *— 1 Thessalonians 5:11-14 ESV*

Grace: *disposition to or an act or instance of kindness, courtesy, or clemency. — Merriam-Webster Dictionary*

Mercy: *compassion or forbearance shown especially to an offender or to one subject to one's power. A blessing that is an act of divine favor or compassion. Compassionate treatment of those in distress. — Merriam-Webster Dictionary*

Love is forgiving people for what they have done, no matter if they deserve it or not. Whether they ask for forgiveness or try to atone for their wrong doings. Forgiveness clears away the poison from your heart and allows you to operate more like Jesus. Unforgiveness can cause huge wedges and harden hearts. It's hard to interact and bond authentically when unforgiveness is at work.

REAL LOVE

Bear with each other and forgive one another if any of you has a grievance against someone. Forgive as the Lord forgave you.
— Colossians 3:13 NIV

When you are operating in mercy and grace; and have gotten rid of all bitterness and unforgiveness, caring for people becomes so much easier. Not perfect but easier. Caring for others doesn't just apply to our family and friends; this applies to those in need. As children of God, we are given resources to live but also to bless others. Everyone in this life needs assistance. Sometimes the need is physical. The woman who can't feed all of her children, the homeless man who needs warm clothes for the winter, the orphanage in Africa that needs clean water for its children. Everyone has a prayer and is hoping that God will hear and answer them. And the wonderful thing is, He does! He just sends His children as the mail carriers to deliver the blessings.

"A kind gesture can reach a wound that only compassion can heal." — Steve Maraboli, Life, the Truth, and Being Free

We are to be ambassadors for Christ while on earth. That means being His tangible hands and feet. It means being the physical mail carriers of answered prayers. As we learn to love God, we learn to love ourselves in a more authentic way. And the more we love ourselves, the easier it is to love others.

I want to encourage you today that love is possible, it is real, and it surpasses even our wildest imaginations. It is better than any song or movie can depict. But you will only truly experience it by learning to love and receive love from the Father. And if you need some help with what to do, check out the book of Deuteronomy in the Bible for some insight.

Arise, my love,
My beautiful companion and run with me to the higher place. For now is the time to arise and come away with me. For you are my dove, hidden in the split-open rock. It was I who took you and hid you up high in the secret stairway of the sky. Let me see your radiant face and hear your sweet voice. How beautiful your eyes of worship and lovely your voice in prayer. — Song of Songs 2:13-14 TPT

Your Father, God

Prayer

Father God,

I desire to be loved and to love. I desire to experience love Your way. Renew my mind Lord; and change my definition of love. As I learn to love You more, I pray that my love for myself will grow. And as I love myself, that my capacity to love others will expand. Help me to obey you and give with a cheerful heart. Exchange my heart of stone for a heart of flesh.

In Jesus' name,
Amen.

Love Moment

1. Write down your perception of what love is. Then write down two scriptures about love. Compare your idea of love with the truth of God's love. Spend time meditating on what the Bible says love is so that it becomes your new normal.
2. Make a self-care schedule where you do something just for you once a month. If you already have a couple self-care practices, add a daily affirmation, or do something new.
3. Intentionally go out of your way to do something nice for someone else: Pay for the meal of the person behind you in the fast food lane, send a random "thinking of you" card, and compliment another lady you see walking by.

_____
_____
_____
_____
_____
_____
_____
_____
_____
_____
_____

In Your infinite power, You made me...
With earth and pieces of Your personality You determined who I'd be...
A messy project turned to a masterpiece.
A creative installation for Your glory, for all the world to see.
A lighthouse-built brick by brick from the traumas that tried to break me.
You're raising me.
Showing me the very essence of love:
A firm hand, distinct voice, and arms in which I can always run to.

For Your son, who died and made
this all possible was the first to
show us how real Your love is.
Chasing away the shadows and
breathing us back to life...
Back to light – for we are made in
Your image...
Your whispers are sweet kisses
that I am drawn to.
Every sign or word from Heaven
leaves me in awe that You see me...
Not the mask, You see me nakedly:
The insecurities, the impatience,
the distrust, and the fear of hope
being broken...

The daughter overworked,
overlooked, and virtue stolen...
You saw me...And called me
beautiful.
You saw me, as a masterpiece, the
Holy Spirit Your utensil.
And loved me until I began to shine
with the light of Your love.
You took an ordinary girl and
proclaimed her Queen.
Adopted forever into Your lineage,
You, the King of Kings.
My heart sings in response to the
nearness of You.
And I long to show others of what
real love can do,

When real love meets the thirsty at
the well of uncertainties and sin.
THAT is where real love begins.
And I for one am thankful You
chose me to be both lover and
friend,
Daughter and servant...
Forever grateful to experience a
love that knows no end.

Treasure Box

"When our eyes see our hands doing the work of our hearts, the circle of Creation is completed inside us, the doors of our souls fly open, and love steps forth to heal everything in sight."
– Michael Bridge

In this day and age, we give so much of ourselves away. Our time, our talent, our love, our emotions … our bodies. And more often than not, we give away pieces of ourselves to people who have no real desire to invest in them but rather rent them for a desired time period. And the pieces we give away are never returned in the same condition.

We focus more on what we can do for people so that they will accept us versus being ourselves and welcoming those who appreciate it. The world counts lies, views, and money stacks, but who we are is where the real value lies. Many will argue about which part of us holds the most worth, but I am here to tell you it is your heart.

And being in Bethany in the house of Simon the leper, as he sat at meat, there came a woman having an alabaster box of ointment of spikenard very precious; and she brake the box, and poured it on his head. And Jesus said, Let her alone; why trouble ye her? she hath wrought a good work on me. – Mark 14:3, 6 KJV

Although people talk about the box, I have come to find that it was what was inside that held the real value. And the sacrifice of her pouring it out meant nothing without the giving of herself. It was her heart and mind posture that made it all special.

Anyone can theoretically earn money and buy presents. We all have gifts and talents. We are not the first, nor the last to receive the various promotions. To hang that certificate or degree on the wall. But the one thing that can never be duplicated is your one-of-a-kind heart.

It is the heart that stirs up the courage to protect those we love.

It is the heart that causes us to look for love.

It was the desire of the heart that conquered countries and won wars.

It is the condition of our heart that ultimately leads us towards Jesus.

Above all else, guard your heart, for everything you do flows from it. – Proverbs 4:23 NIV

All of our motives, wants, desires start first in the heart and then our brains move to strategize the plan to accomplish those desires. We know that our hearts were important to God. The heart is mentioned 963 times in the King James Version and 791 times in the New International Version. And it, the part we protect and care for the least.

Treasure: *noun; something of great worth or value. A person esteemed as rare or precious.* **Treasured; Treasuring**: *verb; to hold or keep as precious: cherish, prize*
– Merriam-Webster Dictionary

If we were honest, how many of us look at our hearts as treasure? As something sacred, of extreme value or importance? Understanding as beautiful as it is, it is fragile. It is the very core of who we are. A rare gem we treat like a punching bag in a gym, anyone can take a swing. And we wonder why our ability to love, trust, and connect on a deeper intimate level is difficult. Why we are left wanting. Why God can seem so far away.

TREASURE BOX

At Jesus' feet

At Jesus' feet

At mercy's seat

There, where all my weaknesses

And His strength finally meet.

Secrets unfold

I pour out my soul

My weary soul's retreat

It is here at my Jesus' feet.

— Billy Gaines

After many failed attempts at relationships, I cried out to God, enough was enough. From the relationships when I was trying to find myself in high school to the many in college when I lost myself. I had spent the last 15 years searching for love in men who I thought really cared for me ... Men I hoped had the capacity to help me heal my heart wounds. But they didn't. And each relationship, situationship, friend with benefits caused my treasure to break a little more. Being sexually assaulted as a freshman in college while a virgin. Falling in love, getting pregnant as a sophomore, and choosing to have an abortion; just to be dumped the very next morning. Love for me, in my adult years, had me eyeing the end of a bottle and ready to fight anyone who was trying to take the "love" I was fighting to keep away. Love was a high-priced commodity I never had trouble giving but never seemed to receive in return.

In December 2017, in a sea of tears, I gave God my treasure. I was on E. Like a car with no gas trying to make it to the next gas station. I was on my last leg. Having gone through the gauntlet of dissolving my longest relationship with my son's father, I was ready to retreat. This beautiful box with a fragile gem inside - my heart. I knew only God would know what to do with it and how to put it back together. I admitted that while I had so much love to give, it was obvious, that I didn't know the value of my own heart or how to truly care for it. I realized that what took the longest to repair wasn't my finances, what hurt the most wasn't having to move and start a new life; it was the recovery of my heart. And each heartbreak, weighed more heavily than the last. Humbly, I asked God to keep my heart until He found one worthy of stewarding it.

Our hearts tend to be that one room in the house that never gets cleaned up. No, we just keep stuffing the junk in and sweeping right outside the door to make it look pretty. We put on these fancy masks of blessed and highly favored when we are broken and in desperate need of repair. But if we are honest, we are afraid. Afraid to take inventory of our heart and to accept the responsibility of its condition. So, we shut the doors and throw away the key. We dream wonderful fantasies and never experience the real thing. Like a car in neutral we are stuck going nowhere.

"Your vision will become clear only when you look into your heart ... Who looks outside, dreams. Who looks inside, awakens." – Carl Jung

The real talk is often we value the external pieces of ourselves more than the internal. We have regiments and products for everything people can see but the very thing that brings life into our bodies we ignore. We give our hearts and bodies away without taking the time to inspect the character and intentions of men. We move from relationship to relationship looking for love but don't take time to love on ourselves first. We turn our noses up at the price of therapy and self-improvement programs but will drop thousands on shoes, hair, and food that is temporary. The gift of you has nothing to do with any of those material things but in who you are. God desires the one thing we seem to value the least: our hearts. Sweet sisters, you can have an authentic relationship with God and interact with Him on a higher level as you desire. You just have to willingly give your heart to Him. Raw, broken, and messy. Always the perfect gentleman, He will never force or coerce you. He waits patiently for you to give it to Him - withholding nothing.

It's time to wake up.

TREASURE BOX

My sweet sisters, I want to encourage you today to offer your heart to God. We have tried it our way, numerous times. And each time we failed to receive what we were looking for. But there is one who is strong enough, committed enough, loving enough to give us what we need. Today as you say this prayer, really choose to give God a chance with managing the treasure of your heart. He will never leave you nor forsake you.

Prayer

Father God,

I admit that I have not taken good care of my
heart. I have lent it to the wrong people and
underestimated its importance and worth.
Lord, I place my treasure box, I place my heart
in Your hands. As the One who created me,
that is the safest place. Heal my heart and hold
it until You find one worthy of caring for it.
And help me to learn how to care for it better.

In Jesus' name,
Amen.

Love Moment

As you pray this prayer, envision yourself placing your treasure box - the representation of your heart into God's hands. Feel free to write or draw what you see. What is your treasure box like? This makes it more personal to you. And for those who dream or have visions, you are likely to see it again!

Trust Spelled Like Faith

Trust is the first step to love. – Munshi Premchand

Trust: *Firm belief in the reliability, truth, ability, or strength of someone or something. – Merriam-Webster Dictionary*

The hardest thing is to rebuild trust once it is broken. It's like a crystal vase, once it's broken, you can repair it but it's not quite what it used to be. Some of the pieces are missing and it's more fragile than before. And each time it gets damaged, it becomes more and more unrecognizable.

For many of us, broken trust didn't start in our adult lives, it started when we were children. From the various forms of abuse, rejection, and abandonment we grow up with fragmented trust. And then we enter romantic relationships. The vase shatters.

We deceive ourselves and "get by" as we continue to form friendships and relationships. Yet there is a level in us that people can never quite touch. Why? Because of trust. It's like inviting people into your home and restricting them only to the living room and kitchen. They only get to experience a small piece of a beautiful mansion called your heart.

And then we are found by God. We attempt to apply the same rules of engagement unknowingly and yet it doesn't work. Life hits and we need Him but have only allowed Him into certain areas of our hearts

Behold, I'm standing at the door, knocking. If your heart is open to hear my voice and you open the door within, I will come in to you and feast with you, and you will feast with me.
– Revelation 3:20 TPT

58

TRUST SPELLED LIKE FAITH

Sweet sisters, we will never experience the fullness of God's love without trust. A lot of the time, people relegate trust to big tangible things: a house, marriage, money, sickness, and world peace. Don't get me wrong, we all desire these things. But for God, your treasure is your heart. And so He wants us to trust Him to love us and journey in learning to love Him authentically - with all your heart.

> **Faith**: *complete trust or confidence in someone or something. Strong belief in God or in the doctrines of a religion, based on spiritual apprehension rather than proof. – Merriam-Webster Dictionary*

Now faith is the substance of things hoped for, the evidence of things not seen. – Hebrews 11:1 NKJV

The hardest thing about trust is that it starts with faith. For many of us, healthy trust is a foreign concept. We do not have experience to draw from, to put our trust in. So we have to hope and believe in what the Word says but we have yet to experience.

Like trusting enough to let it go. As the oldest of five girls, I was the "second mom." I cooked, cleaned, and babysat my siblings starting in the 5th grade. That was life. It intensified when my parents separated when I was 16 and then divorced the following year. I had to be the strong one. I always was. And being five years older than my next sibling, I often felt alone. We were always in different stages of life. When I was in middle school, they were in elementary. When I was in high school, they were in middle and elementary school. And so on. I never had anyone to talk about puberty with, crushes on boys, heartbreaks, and frustrations. And as the oldest child, outside of school, I was always in the house watching my sisters. Then add on the fights with my parents as I was finding myself as a pre-teen and teenager, that was icing on the cake. Episodes of bad communication, silent treatments, and anger ending in tears was my norm. So I grew up learning to stuff my feelings inside and not sharing the important pieces of myself. I retreated so far within myself, by my senior year of high school I had taught myself how to suppress my tears by the count of three. Never would I allow someone to know how they hurt me willingly. I would be a fortress, unbreakable.

Icebox where my heart used to be.

As a teenage girl, I conditioned myself not to cry. Obviously, it wasn't flawless, but I had disciplined myself to internalize pain and control my outward appearance. Due to past traumas, I had decided I would not allow people to see that they had hurt me. That way they wouldn't know how vulnerable I was ... Or how to hurt me in the future. And so this sweet 16 year old conditioned herself to stop crying by the time she counted to three. And for the most part it worked.

As I tried to open up in relationships, with each one failing, more bricks were added to fortify the walls of my heart. I was like that for years, wanting to love and be loved, but never allowing someone inside. Never allowing someone to really experience me or for me to experience the liveliness of emotions. I came to a point in my first year of singleness after the long-term relationship where I could feel God tapping on my heart. In prayer and worship, I could feel the emotions coming to the surface, but could I trust Him? Could I trust Him enough to really let my guard down and allow my heart to breathe for once? Could I trust Him with the pieces...? That He would do what His Word says and put them back together? Would He genuinely love this version of me? Would He truly lovingly accept me with all my junk or smite me for my imperfections? Please excuse me, I have a flare for dramatics. I admit it, I fought it for a while. But one day I took a chance, I wanted more. I wanted the love of a Father that the Bible talked about that I never had. I wanted a safe place. I wanted someone to love me. So, I did the unthinkable, I took a chance and I ugly cried.

Now may God, the inspiration and foundation of hope, fill you to overflowing with uncontainable joy and perfect peace as you trust in him. And may the power of the Holy Spirit continually surround your life with his super-abundance until you radiate with hope! – Romans 15:13 TPT

TRUST SPELLED LIKE FAITH

Daughters of God, the Word says we go from faith to faith. That means there are levels in this journey. God wants to authentically get to know you. That means, sharing your heart and laying your hurts and pains at His feet; it means allowing Him to be your protector, your counselor, and your friend. But that takes trust! It takes giving God a chance even though you may not have a track record of His goodness - yet.

> *Know therefore that the Lord your God, He is God, the faithful God, who keeps His covenant and His lovingkindness to a thousandth generation with those who love Him and keep His commandments. – Deuteronomy 7:9 NASB*

I want to encourage you to try. It may seem very hard at first. You may feel silly … You may feel nothing and think your efforts are in vain. They are not! Although we journey to the same destination, our feet will not take the same path. But God is faithful, and He walks each of us all the way through. I am confident that you will find after a while that you long for those moments. When the Father is able to wrap you in peace and love. When the sweetness of His presence causes time to fly by. When you are worshipping and awaken from a peaceful sleep.

God is knocking at the door of your heart. Will you let Him in?

Prayer

Father God,

Help me learn how to trust You. I believe and hope in all the promises that Your Word says about Your love and Your faithfulness. When You come knocking, give me the courage to let You in. No restrictions. I pray that You will meet in a tangible way that my faith in trust in You would continuously grow. I desire our relationship to grow on a deeper level.

In Jesus' name,
Amen.

Love Moment

In your time of worship and prayer allow the Holy Spirit to lead and guide you. If you feel emotions coming to the surface, be courageous and journey through them with God. If He brings memories or a person to mind, choose to reflect and process what is taking place or took place versus pushing the thoughts away. Journal your experiences. Take note of how you felt at the beginning and at the end of your time with God.

_____
_____
_____
_____
_____
_____
_____
_____
_____
_____
_____
_____
_____
_____
_____
_____
_____

In To Me See

"All intimacy is rare—that's what makes it precious. And it involves the revelation of one's self and the loving gaze upon another's true self. Intimacy requires honesty and kindness in almost equal measure, trust, and trustworthiness, forgiveness and the capacity to be forgiven." – Amy Bloom

This is probably one of the least fun subjects, but critical to our relationship with God: Intimacy. Society, entertainment, and social media would have us believe that intimacy is having sex or being romantic. It's not true. These things are just vehicles to create or maintain a level of intimacy.

> **Intimacy:** *the state of being intimate: FAMILIARITY. Something of a personal or private nature. Intimate:*
> *1a: marked by a warm friendship developing through long association*
> *intimate friends*
> *1b: suggesting informal warmth or privacy*
> *2: of a very personal or private nature*
> *3: marked by very close association, contact, or familiarity*
> *– Merriam-Webster Dictionary*

True intimacy in a relationship is opening up and expressing exactly what you feel. The good, the bad, and the ugly. There is a level of trust that most of us are too afraid to have when it comes to those feelings. The enemy uses our relationships when we are young to distort our idea or comfortability with intimacy. Through our relationships with family and friends, our trust is betrayed. We are rejected and let down. Our emotions are often discounted. And so, we pull ourselves inward more and more. We become great pretenders.

Able to hold conversations while being full of pain inside. We learn to smile while the world is falling apart because we have been tricked that no one will really be there. No one will really care. And so when this great big loving God comes, we aren't sure what to do. We have questions in our hearts that we would never dare to say because "It's blasphemy!" The truth is we get so bogged down mentally by all the internal questions, "Will this make them leave? Will they still love me if they find out?" And so instead of having gates to guard our hearts, we have walls that keep everyone else out and keep us trapped inside.

The great thing is…God never will leave. He will never forsake you.

God is not afraid of your bad. Your weakness, your tears, or the pain you try your best not to let anyone see. The beautiful thing about God is, that's the part of you He wants to love on the most.

But it takes strength – it takes courage to be more honest and truthful than you typically are…even with yourself.

Sharing the ugly.

"He didn't know what to do, but his instincts, his blind rage, the surge of revulsion at what this bully had done, his fear, his pent-up emotions, all spilled over, and he attacked like a cornered animal, gouging, pulling, kicking, punching." – Peter Heller

The animal backed into the corner? Yea, that was me. I was a talkative, smart-aleck, and super hardheaded child. I admit I definitely gave my parents the blues to a degree. Well, as hardheaded as I was, the punishments were harder. My father was the disciplinarian of the house and heavy was his hand. Moments that started as discipline often ended as an outlet for anger. And ironically, as much tenacity as I had, I wasn't a fighter. It wasn't my nature. And that is not good when you hit the fourth and fifth grade of elementary school.

For whatever reason, I had become the target at school and on the bus. I had gotten into two fights with boys and was bullied by girls. It got so bad, everyone who got off at my stop followed me home. There were numerous times when my mom would look out the window and see me trying not to cry as I walked up the driveway. Well, my dad had had enough. After that day, my dad started to fight me every day. Six foot two inches tall versus maybe four foot three inches. I cannot tell you how long this went on, but it was absolute hell. Between having to fight a giant in my eyes and dealing with the discipline, it was too much.

One day I snapped and started swinging back. He thought the exercises had done the trick, but in reality, what it - coupled with the discipline - produced was so much more and so much worse. I have had a pan thrown at my head because I wasn't understanding my math homework and welts from an extension cord because I thought I was fat in the fourth grade and wouldn't eat my lunch. I have been choked almost until unconsciousness for rolling my eyes. By high school, I was a raging mess on the inside and if you shook the soda bottle long enough, I would explode and take anyone and everyone with me.

I was angry with God. I was mad at the world for a very long time. Where there should have been a developing lioness, there was a mouse who didn't know who she was. A woman who didn't even know she had experienced trauma and needed help. And it was something I was afraid to share. I had been crying to the Lord for identity but was unwilling to confront the very strongholds that were holding me hostage. But you can only go but so deep with God when you have darkness on the inside that you're unwilling to confront.

Why God???

Why did this have to happen to me???

Why didn't You stop it????

WHY DID YOU LET THIS HAPPEN????

I'M SO ANGRY!!!!!!!!!

I couldn't see how all of this could be used for my good. How is my brokenness good? How could the rage on the inside of me produce something beautiful? How could God say He loved me but abandon me? This is the ugly no one gets to see, and we aren't brave enough to discuss with the King.

And as transparent as I can be, even now it's hard to go back there. To relive the moments and feel what I felt. But doing the work with God over the years makes this moment possible. Not pleasant, but possible. I said to the Lord, when He gave me this part of my story to share, "I don't want to go here, but I will be obedient. I need You to help me."

Ugly. When the emotions are in their rawest state. It means facing the memories that have haunted you for years. It means trusting Him with your tears and believing He won't leave you there alone. It's not just about the pain, but also acknowledging your struggles and discussing it with God in the moment. Bad money management, addictions, and lust.

The call to purity.

It is God's will that you should be sanctified: that you should avoid sexual immorality; that each of you should learn to control your own body in a way that is holy and honorable, not in passionate lust like the pagans, who do not know God.
– 1 Thessalonians 4:3-5 NIV

When I made my life change in 2017, one of the things I committed to God was my purity. That I would walk in purity and exercise abstinence until I was married. The struggle is real sisters. Especially after you have been sexually active. It was easy for me not to have sex because I wasn't dating anyone. But what about masturbating? Watching porn? Many of us don't like to talk about it but we engage in these activities. And it was a super hard habit and stronghold to break. Over the course of a year, I had to learn to be vulnerable with God in a way that I had never known. When I was struggling the most, to literally ask Him to help me because in about three seconds, I was going to give in. And on my days when I fell, promptly going to Him for forgiveness so that there was no distance between us. That is typically when the enemy is able to send us further from God with seeds of condemnation. And don't get me started on when you start talking to someone after a period of isolation. Lawd, those parts of you awaken with a vengeance if you don't put proper boundaries and safeguards in place!

In the midst of tears, telling God you don't understand the whys of a situation…

Telling him even how you may dislike yourself…the ugly! "Too fat, too short, too tall, too skinny… If I looked like this… If I was smart like her…" It's not easy but there is freedom in truth! By acknowledging it – to yourself and God, you take the power out of it…there are no hidden skeletons in the closet because we have already laid everything at His feet.

Being honest isn't easy, many times I ended up in tears because I realized the weight of what I was confessing and what it really meant. I had to look in the mirror of how I really felt about myself and allow God to come in and fill me with his positive affirmations and love.

And that's the part right? Allowing someone close enough to touch those parts of you that may be painful to touch. Where disappointment and rejection have left wounds, real love comes to heal them.

Beauty for ashes, that's His promise to us. But it is an exchange. God is not a bulldozer; He is a gentleman. So, He waits for us to invite Him into the secret parts so He can heal our wounds and open our eyes and ears to who He has called us to be.

"Behold, I'm standing at the door, knocking. If your heart is open to hear my voice and you open the door within, I will come into you and feast with you, and you will feast with me."
– Revelation 3:20 TPT

I get it, this is not an easy task. But it is one that can change your whole life.

"Are you weary, carrying a heavy burden? Then come to me. I will refresh your life, for I am your oasis. Simply join your life with mine. Learn my ways and you'll discover that I'm gentle, humble, and easy to please. You will find refreshment and rest in me. For all I require of you will be pleasant and easy to bear." – Matthew 11:28-30 TPT

Opening up to God and allowing Him in will never be a bad investment. He will not betray your trust or neglect you... He understands the worth of your heart; that's why He's jealous about you.

Be brave and courageous, choose to open the door and let ABBA in. Your life will never be the same.

Prayer

Father God,

I desire an intimate fulfilling relationship with You. Help me to boldly accept your invitation when You come. Father, when You show me things about myself that are not pleasing to You, help me to not fall into condemnation but to see that You are a loving parent trying to help me to get back into alignment with You. To be who You've called me to be. Lord, help me to be brave as You uncover the areas of my heart that are hurting the most. I thank You for Your promise of beauty for my ashes. Help me to lay my baggage at Your feet. I pray Father, that as I learn to be intimate with You, that I will become more authentic and establish deeper relationships with the people You have placed in my life. I thank You that Your presence is a safe place and somewhere I am always welcome.

In Jesus' name,
Amen.

Love Moment

In your time of prayer and devotion, be honest about what you feel with God. Surrender to the emotions He may be drawing out of you, don't try to stuff them down. When He points out something in your character that needs to change, do not distance yourself from the Father. Instead, meditate on what He has shown you and ask Him for His divine assistance (clean hands, pure heart, and a renewed right spirit).

Write what you feel in a journal entry to God. This is just about being authentic about what's bothering you, the things you fear, how you feel about yourself, etc. Note any signs, messages, or songs He sends to you in response.

Believe He will respond.

_____
_____
_____
_____
_____
_____
_____
_____
_____
_____
_____

Forgiveness is Freedom

Forgiveness releases us, Intercession covers them.

One thing we often want to overlook and not deal with is forgiveness. But as our Abba opens our hearts and begins the surgery and healing process, there is only so far you can go without forgiveness.

> **Forgiveness:** *the intentional and voluntary process by which a victim undergoes a change in feelings and attitude regarding an offense and overcomes negative emotions such as resentment and vengeance (however justified it might be). – Merriam-Webster*

There are many hurts and pains that we have from our past. And if we were honest, we still are looking for payment from those who are at fault. We want them to know how we feel, what was lost, the time, energy, love, money, and resources that were given without return. But part of our healing is God forgiving our own sins. Wiping the slate clean so we can begin again.

Remember, God is true to His Word. And the Word has much to say about forgiveness:

> *The Lord our God is merciful and forgiving, even though we have rebelled against him. – Daniel 9:9 NIV*

The hard truth my sisters, is that we fail to realize that by trying to hold our offenders responsible, we hold ourselves hostage. You cannot go forward while holding on to the past. It's like a tug of war that never goes anywhere. And all that happens is you remain stagnant and depleted of energy. In freeing your accuser, you free yourself.

FORGIVENESS IS FREEDOM

"A rattlesnake, if cornered, will become so angry it will bite itself. That is exactly what the harboring of hate and resentment against others is -- a biting of oneself. We think we are harming others in holding these spites and hates, but the deeper harm is to ourselves."
– E. Stanley Jones

... forgive those who trespassed against us.

My father was one of the most important people I had to forgive. The truth was as harmful as our relationship was, I wanted his love. I was angry, volatile, and very lost. I had no sense of identity and I was trying to find it in our limited interactions and broken relationship ... In between the elephants in the room. And one day, the Lord told me I had to let the relationship die. I had to let it go. It was so hard but needed. By taking a step back, God could come in and show me the truth. By letting the relationship die and all its disappointments and expectations, He could clear the clutter and prepare a space for something new to be built.

It was in that time period, that I was able to see my father for who he was: a human man made up of several choices that he was both happy with and regretted. That he, just like I, was a parent who had been trying to find his way in adulthood while caring for a child with no manual. Had I not too made mistakes as a mom? Had selfish moments? Said things I regretted in moments of irritation or being emotional? I had. Had I given the enemy an open door through those moments of fear, unhealed hurts, and anger? Yes, I had. And it was from there, that the Lord helped me to take my dad down from this unrealistic pedestal and see him correctly. And therefore forgive.

Let all bitterness and wrath and anger and clamor and slander be put away from you, along with all malice. Be kind to one another, tender-hearted, forgiving each other, just as God in Christ also has forgiven you. – Ephesians 4:31-32 NASB

Now please do not misunderstand. I am in no way excusing a behavior or words that you received or experienced. There are things I experienced that I may never know the reason behind. That's not what forgiveness is about. Forgiveness is saying, "Lord, I am not the judge, You are. I leave them and their deeds in Your hands." Romans 12:19 in the New King James Version states, "beloved, do not avenge yourselves, but *rather* give place to wrath; for it is written, Vengeance *is* Mine, I will repay," says the Lord. God's got it! But we have to leave it truly in His hands. And what His vengeance will be for each person? That's not for us to know! The important thing is to rest assured that He will handle it, we just need to let go.

I Forgive Me.

Whew. While we hold court for others that have offended us, we ignore the elephant in the room. We literally are holding a grand trial against ourselves. No bail. Outside of what others have done to us, there are many mistakes and consequences we've had to pay because of our own decisions. And though we may learn and move on in wisdom, we are still subconsciously punishing ourselves. A part of ourselves is locked up in the jail of our hearts and minds. And every time we truly make a conscious effort to move on, the rap sheet of offenses starts to replay in our mind. It causes fear, insecurity, and stagnation. We cannot enjoy the freedom that God has for us because the chain of our past is holding us back.

I'll be honest, sweet sisters, forgiving myself is something I still very much battle with. Hindsight truly being 20/20, there are many things I wish I could have done differently. I still wrestle with all the bad financial decisions I made – student loans, multiple credit cards, putting a significant other on my credit, and the many times I wasted money on things that don't even matter or exist right now. I wrestle with not using my time in college wisely. Instead of being head over heels for boys, I wish I had studied abroad, taken trips, networked with more people. Instead, I was carrying my son in his carrier to and from classes so I could finish school.

I wrestle with the fact that I had my son out of wedlock. That he is growing up without the complete family unit experience. Especially since that was the one thing I vowed to never do after experiencing my parents' divorce. The guilt and shame I feel when it's hard to make ends meet, or moments when he's alone because we are a single-family household and I have to work, my heart drops. Especially during COVID-19. I wonder how life could be now if I had made different decisions. But the truth is, I'll never know. And constantly looking back to analyze what can never be changed hinders me from seeing all the beautiful things God is doing in my life now and the wonderful blessings that are on the horizon.

God is not seeking punishment or payment from us. That is what the sacrifice of His Son was for. So why do we? All He wants us to do is repent, turn away from the actions that grieve Him, and walk in the grace of each new day. He chose and chooses to give us new life every day, in spite of what we've done. It's time to unlock the cages - the prisons in which we hold ourselves in through unforgiveness and fly free.

I'm sorry.

As children, we were taught to say we're sorry. When we said unkind things, refused to share, or were just downright mean; our parents and caretakers held us accountable. Somewhere, in between adolescence and adulthood we forgot to ask for forgiveness. We forgot that we should right our wrongs and come clean. Instead, proudly, we convince ourselves how others deserve the treatment. We highlight their wrongs as justification to why our wrongs are okay. We even petition the courts of Heaven for God to avenge us while using "Jesus knows my heart" as a get out of jail free card.

God sees, knows, and hears all. And our all-knowing Father is not deceived nor amused. We have to begin seeking to resolve and make amends for the things that we have done. Just as a sincere apology is healing to our hearts, the same applies to those whom we hurt!

> *If we confess our sins, he is faithful and just and will forgive us*
> *our sins and purify us from all unrighteousness.*
> *– 1 John 1:9 NIV*

I have many memories that I've hidden in the corners of my mind when I gave tit for tat. Moments when I was jealous and wished

I had someone else's life. The times when I betrayed a friend because I was angry and felt that they didn't value me. How many times had I gossiped and spread rumors without any regard to the damage I was inflicting into other people's lives? And somehow, with all of this in my own "file," I was constantly presenting God theirs.

God will hold those who hurt you accountable, but He holds you accountable as well. Remember, He is no respecter of persons. In God's eyes, what is good for the goose is good for the gander and He weighs our hearts, motives, and actions accordingly.

So, we must acknowledge our faults and humbly ask God to forgive our sins. But the process isn't over, we must then move to life change through repentance.

Seal it with a change.

Repentance helps to stop the cycle of sin and move forward in aligning yourself with Christ.

> *Repent, then, and turn to God, so that your sins may be wiped out, that times of refreshing may come from the Lord.*
> *– Acts 3:19 NIV*

Repentance is the difference between lip service and real-life change. How many of you have ever tried to diet? More than likely, the results were temporary or none. Why? Because our "why," our dedication to change was surface level. But when we chose to make a lifestyle change, when our resolve was strong enough, we began to lose weight. Repentance follows the same principle. We must start with asking for forgiveness, acknowledging that we have sinned against God. And then, out of love and respect, move to change. When we release others through prayer and ourselves through repentance, we get to experience something that we all desire: freedom.

> **Freedom:** *The power or right to act, speak, or think as one wants without hindrance or restraint. Absence of subjection to foreign domination.*

FORGIVENESS IS FREEDOM

Real forgiveness removes the poison from within you. It gives us the freedom to start new without the constraints of the pain from the past. Many of us only become halfway free because the second part truly requires bravery. The courage to open your heart again. To put yourself out there, make friends, find love... But not from the perspective of protection or fear. But of grace, mercy, and love. That's the hard part and the key to true forgiveness.

> *Let love and faithfulness never leave you; bind them around your neck, write them on the tablet of your heart. Then you will win favor and a good name in the sight of God and man.*
> *—Proverbs 3:3-4*

In our pursuit of an authentic relationship with God, unforgiveness is not an option! Turning away from sin is not an option! Sisters let's not just forgive others but free ourselves...completely.

Prayer

Father God,

Thank You for your mercy and grace. It is only because of your unconditional love through the sacrifice of Jesus Christ that I am able to be forgiven by You. I acknowledge Your command to forgive others and I ask that You give me the strength to do so. Lord, help me to place them at Your feet and leave them there, knowing that vengeance is Yours and You will repay. As I release them, I thank You for releasing me.

In Jesus' name,
Amen.

Love Moment

On a blank piece of paper, write the name of the person or people who have done you wrong. Write, next to each name, the form of payment you are looking for and the amount of it. Then, with a red pen or marker write in large letters across the paper: **ALL DEBTS PAID!**

An example is on the next page. If you can't do step 2, it's okay... That's part of realizing the truth. They really can't honestly pay it back! But **most importantly**, say a prayer for them.

Bonus: Look at yourself in the mirror and say, "I forgive me," and add why.

_____
_____
_____
_____
_____
_____
_____
_____
_____
_____
_____
_____
_____

Records & Registration of Heart & Soul

Name: _____   Payment Due Date: _____
                              New Balance: _____
                              Minimum Due: _____

PAST DUE

This is an attempt to collect a debt, and any information obtained will be used for that purpose.

Name	Offense	Price

00X00MATTHEW18:2122KJV70X

Records & Registration of Heart & Soul

Payment Amount:

Please make all payments payable to _____.

Payments are accepted in the form of _____.

Worship

"Worship is the subjection of the personality of the worshipper to the object worshipped; it is therefore the affirmation of the relations the two personalities bear to one another."
– Sabrine Baring-Gould

Worship. We've seen it on television, social media, and in the church. Pastors invite us to stand and worship the Lord. Have you ever thought to yourself "what does that really mean?" Or "how do I do that?" I know I have. Have you ever been singing the songs with the congregation but felt like you were missing out? That whatever was happening, it wasn't quite clicking for you? Me too, sis, me too.

Worship is a way to show love. It is beautiful and unique. It brings you into the wonderful presence of God. But in order to authentically worship - we must have a real understanding of what it is before we can truly operate in its fullness. Let's first start with the definition.

> **Worship:** noun – *The feeling or expression of reverence and adoration for a deity; verb – Show reverence and adoration for (a deity), honor with religious rites. – Merriam-Webster*

Worship takes time! Many times, we see the choir or worship team take the stage and just go! And as the audience, we are in awe at how quickly the presence of God fills the room. But the part we do not see is the personal/team worship and prayer that happens beforehand in preparation for the service.

Often, because of this, we get discouraged when we try to worship in our own homes because it doesn't look or feel the same. Worship or true adoration and even love cannot be microwaved. It takes time to remove all the wandering thoughts, to silence the voice of stress and fear to truly focus on loving God. You may find that it takes 4-5 songs before you feel a shift in the atmosphere. But I promise you, dear sisters, if you search for Him, He <u>will</u> show up!

You will seek me and find me when you seek me with all your heart. – Jeremiah 29:13 NIV

We must worship in spirit and in truth (John 4:24 NKJV). A big part of that is worshipping in the truth of who you are and not mimicking what other people do. It's so personal! Like a love letter or a homemade card, a 6-year-old gives to their father. It will sometimes look the same as the standard worship we see in church and other times it will not. Your declaration of love is unique and that's okay! God loves that about you! Never for a minute allow the enemy to come in and deter you from worship because of the false standard that he wants us to ascribe to. You don't have to be the worship leader, you don't have to be loud, you don't have to shout, jump around, etc. How you display your love is completely up to you, it just must be from your heart.

Tears like rain.

Talk about learning your worship love language of crying. How ironic is that! During Sunday services I would struggle to stay in the "spirit" because I didn't want to emote. Finally, the glass ceiling broke.

I had been going to church faithfully for a couple of years but now I was learning to spend time with God alone at home. I would feel Him calling me to worship and so I would sing. But there was a problem. I could feel the dams in my heart bursting to open up. And it was beginning to manifest in tears. So I would stop singing. I would try to collect myself so that I could continue to "worship" God. How ironic. I had only really known tears in a bad way, it never occurred to me that I could experience happy tears.

I needed to embrace the fact that tears are a part of my worship! They are the physical manifestation of what I feel for God on the inside. But because of my past and lack of healing, I was hindering myself from authentically worshipping God. I was only allowing myself to come to the edge of vulnerability and intimacy with Him. Where I was comfortable. In order for me to truly worship God, I had to come to a place of understanding and trust. God is a safe place! It was ok to show my emotions and to be vulnerable because He loved me unconditionally. He would never do anything to betray my trust or my heart! And although I had not been able to trust men, He was asking me to place my faith in who the Word said He was.

The closer in proximity to God you are, everything that is not like Him cannot stand.

I think you all know me well enough by now to know it wasn't overnight. It took a while for me to surrender. To be vulnerable in my adoration to Him. But He was patient. And in time, I did. It was the most freeing thing to be able to express my joys, my pain, my hope, my disappointments, and my love for God. *Withholding nothing.* And now, I freely give Him my tears of adoration and love. Often, if you could peek into my home, you'd find me a snotty, red-eyed mess! But He's been that good to me and the least that I can do is love on Him as best as I can.

Uncage the bird and let it sing.

Make a joyful shout to the Lord, all you lands! Serve the Lord with gladness; Come before His presence with singing. Enter into His gates with thanksgiving, And into His courts with praise. Be thankful to Him and bless His name.
– Psalm 100: 1-2, 4 NKJV

Although I love to sing, I am not a singer. Yes, as a young teen and young adult, I loved to sing love songs. The shower is my greatest stage, lol. But when I went to church and sang, I tried to hide. There was something about the lilt of my own voice that was daunting. *"I can't sing to the Lord like she did … my voice is nowhere near as good."* And this line of thinking affected my worship. Although at home I had more privacy to explore and discover my worship, there were still things that hindered me. Like the volume of my voice. Y'all, I can be very loud. In my college days, when we "called" to one another, everyone knew the highest and longest skrill was mine. Or with friends, you are apt to hear me laughing loudly. It's never loud for attention but in real moments of comfortability you may hear a very loud laugh or exclamation. But for some reason, my worship had to be "room temperature". And in the dead of night, when people could hear the most, a whisper. I was afraid. 'What if the neighbors hear me? What will they think? Will they laugh if I'm off key? Will they talk about me? What if they decide to file a noise complaint? There was such an insecurity about my voice and what I was not that I did not offer the fullness of my own loving melodies.

Because your love is better than life, my lips will glorify you. I will praise you as long as I live, and in your name, I will lift up my hands. – Psalm 63: 3-4 NIV

Until Easter 2020. Sitting at home with my son during our quarantine isolation, I decided to try to make that Sunday as special as possible. We would worship, watch a sermon, eat a big breakfast, and then finish with dinner at my mom's house. So, as I began to worship God, I felt my voice wanting to get louder. Again, I hit a point of internal conflict. Do I surrender and give the Lord all of me or do I succumb to the fears of others hearing me and what they might think? This was the first time I decided what they may hear, and think does not matter. So, I worshipped the Lord and allowed the melody, cadence, and volume to go where I felt the Spirit lead. This went on for about 10 minutes. And the most beautiful surprise when I finished was my son - who had been quiet - looking at me and saying, "Your voice is beautiful, Mommy." He has heard me sing, squawk, etc. for 11 years. But something in the authenticity of my adoration for God sounded beautiful to him.

All worship is beautiful to God. And just like human parents love the different cards and pictures we make them; He loves our variety too! He made us after all.

Here is a list of different activities that you can do to worship God:
- Play instruments
- Sing

WORSHIP

- Dance
- Write
- Paint
- Sitting quietly in His presence

For me, my worship comes mostly in the form of song and poetry. Remember, as in any relationship, there is the journey of discovery. Love doesn't happen overnight, it's built. The more you spend time in worship … it will become a part of your lifestyle.

As you grow in your relationship with the Father, take time to explore the forms of worship that connect you to Him the most. There is no pressure, enjoy the journey!

Prayer

Father God,

I desire to worship You. To connect with You on a deeper level. Holy Spirit help me to learn what authentic worship is. To worship in spirit and in truth. Help me to understand what that really means. Help me to be comfortable and confident in my voice and personal song. I pray that my worship would be as sweet perfume in the courts of Heaven.

In Jesus' name,
Amen.

Love Moment

Pick a "love" song for the Lord. This means choosing a song that is only about how you feel about Him, not what He can/has/will do for you. Sing it every day for a week. Write down any observations, feelings, or messages you receive.

You may find you begin to wake up with songs playing in your head... Smile! That's the presence of the Lord.

_____
_____
_____
_____
_____
_____
_____
_____
_____
_____
_____
_____
_____
_____
_____
_____
_____
_____
_____
_____

Prayer Closet

*A sacred place, where I can face the worries and stresses of each
day. A place to learn and enjoy Your presence, a moment of time
where earth meets Heaven. A place of love, just me and You. I
sit with my Father, for whom, I make room.*
– Crystal Johnson

The prayer closet is one of the most precious, underrated pieces necessary for a personal relationship with God.

I know what you're thinking. *Why do I need that? I can pray anywhere, anytime.*

I get it. I used to feel the same way. God hears me sitting on my bed, right?

While this is indeed true, there is something about having a secret place.

*But when you pray, go into your room, close the door and pray
to your Father, who is unseen. Then your Father, who sees what
is done in secret, will reward you. – Matthew 6:6 NIV*

Prayer Closet: *A dedicated location where Christians go
alone, in privacy, to spend time in prayer with God.*

I remember when God began to wake me up at 3am. At first, I thought it was a fluke. Maybe I'm just hot … I had to use the bathroom, etc. I would take off a blanket or two, use the bathroom or just end up on social media until I fell back asleep. I'm sure many of you can relate. You think it's insomnia, you wonder what you ate, or even take inventory of what's on your mind. And I'm certain I'm not the only one who ended up on social media scrolling idly. I realized on day three – this was becoming a pattern. Remembering the story of Samuel *(1 Samuel 3)* and how God had been calling to him at night, I decided to try something different. I sat up in the bed and tried to pray. Needless to say; after failing to stay awake multiple nights, I realized I needed another option.

One night I felt God tell me to sit in the closet.

The closet, Lord?

Yes - it's quiet, away from "the world," you can turn on the light without disturbing your son and concentrate.

I pondered this and said "Okay, God. We'll try this out."

I admit the first night was a little odd. I grabbed a pillow from the living room, the Bible, my iPhone (you know they are holy, right?), and a journal. That night I was maybe in there for 20 minutes. I felt so silly. I didn't "feel" anything. There were no "raining fire from Heaven" prayers. No visions or dreams. But if at first, you don't succeed, try, try, try again right?

I have come to find that there are many benefits to having a prayer closet. The first one is intentionality and focus! Although I prefer to sit on my bed, it is too easy for me to get distracted. Whether it's falling asleep, playing on my phone, or getting a snack; there is always something else competing for my attention. With the prayer closet, there is a mental shift that begins to happen when you go in. You know the intent is to spend time with God and so those other little distractions melt away. And the more you do it, the shift happens organically.

Prayer closets foster spiritual growth. It offers a space for you to grow with God without pressure. Who has attended a prayer call or been asked to lead in prayer? Or better yet, ever been in a prayer circle and they ask everyone to pray? By the time they would get to me, I would be so nervous. *What if my prayers don't sound like theirs? I don't know as many scriptures ... I can't speak in tongues ...* Our prayer closet is truly a safe place! God does not judge or mock your efforts, He loves it!! He loves that you are being intentional about spending time and learning His Word. Remember, it's a relationship over religion.

The more you spend time in prayer, the stronger you will become. You will find the courage to pray bold prayers, to intercede for your loved ones and not so fond ones. You will develop an "ear" for the Holy Spirit and follow His leading. No tool or gift is effective if the person wielding it doesn't learn to use it and constantly strive to be a master at it.

Make it personal! I encourage you to put up your prayer requests on the walls and/or door so we can see them. Use sticky pads, colorful pieces of paper. Use different color markers and pens to add some spice. Add flowers or air freshener to make it inviting. Make sure you add scriptures pertaining to those prayer requests or just scriptures that have been resonating with you. You will find that reading them out loud boosts your confidence in prayer and you will begin to remember more scriptures over time. Repetition and writing things down are proven methods to remembering or learning things. And people intentionally invest time to learn more about the things or the people they love. Psalm 119:11 talks about the importance of hiding the Word in our hearts. Knowing the Word will help us to pray more effectively and live biblically so that we do not sin against God. It also helps us learn more about who He is and in turn, who we are.

Prayer closets foster intimacy. You can let down your hair and allow yourself a level of vulnerability you probably would not experience in a public space. It gives you room to be real with God and yourself about your thoughts, feelings, and difficulties. You know what is said there never leaves the room! But the great thing is, as you laid your burdens at God's feet, He moves beyond the room on your behalf.

After a couple of nights sitting in the closet things began to change. I began to hear God more clearly. Devotions and scriptures began to jump off the page. It was as if He picked them specifically for what I was going through at the time or to even just shower me with words of affirmation. I began to recognize His voice more. And that carried with me beyond the closet, but into my everyday moments too.

Sometimes as a Christian, we look for these big overt signs that God is present. That He is speaking. But Abba often doesn't operate like that.

PRAYER CLOSET

*Then He said, "Go out, and stand on the mountain before the
Lord." And behold, the Lord passed by, and a great and strong
wind tore into the mountains and broke the rocks in pieces before
the Lord, but the Lord was not in the wind; and after the wind an
earthquake, but the Lord was not in the earthquake; and after the
earthquake a fire, but the Lord was not in the fire; and after the
fire a still small voice. – 1 Kings 19:11-13 NKJV*

Daughters of the Most High, God isn't looking for perfection,
just a willing heart. Obedience even when it doesn't make sense. He
meets you there and eventually you will see how everything truly is
working together for your good.

Remember, although God is not a human, He is very
relational! Just as you spend time with your mom and/or dad; alone
shooting the breeze and talking about life...enjoying each other's
company; God desires to have that kind of bond with His daughters.
We just have to set the atmosphere (mood/environment) and invite
Him in.

Prayer

Father God,

I dedicate this space to You. Use it as You will. I pray that this space would be a place of growth in my prayer life and relationship with You. I pray that each time I come out of our secret place, I will come out stronger, wiser, free, and healed. Bless this place and fill it with Your holy presence.

In Jesus' name,
Amen.

Love Moment

For one week, designate a place in your home where you will spend time with God. Make sure you bring your journal and Bible with you. Feel free to decorate your space with scriptures, written prayers, etc.

Expect for God to meet you there.

_____

_____

_____

_____

_____

_____

_____

_____

_____

_____

_____

_____

_____

_____

_____

_____

_____

_____

_____

_____

_____

Look for Him

And you will seek Me and find Me, when you search for Me with all your heart. – Jeremiah 29:13 NKJV

Whether you are just starting your journey with the Father or journeying to deepen your relationship, make sure you look for Him. God is not cruel. Do not believe the lies that the enemy may whisper about how what you are doing isn't working or how God is far away.

Expect the Lord to not just show up but exceed your expectations. Know in your heart, that on the receiving end of every prayer, love letter, moment of obedience, or worship song is your Heavenly Father who absolutely adores you.

The key to seeing the Father in your life is understanding that He is in the details! There is no such thing as a coincidence. We must not limit or underestimate God. Truly, He cares about all things concerning you, from the large to the small. Often, we overlook the small blessings as coincidences or just "life." It's not, it's the Creator of the world sending you a gift to brighten your day. You'd be surprised how much He pays attention to the things that burden your heart.

Which of you, if your son asks for bread, will give him a stone? Or if he asks for a fish, will give him a snake? If you, then, though you are evil, know how to give good gifts to your children, how much more will your Father in heaven give good gifts to those who ask him! – Matthew 7:9-11 NIV

The best birthday present ever.

January 17, 2020: It's My Birthday!!!

To be honest, I wasn't super excited about the day. As a winter baby, it's always hard to plan a birthday unless you are traveling. You just never know when a blizzard or sheets of ice hit the streets. I had no money, the harvest from all the bad financial decisions over the years had come. I was barely making ends meet with all the debt I had. And so, in an effort to get it together, I was on a very strict budget with very little wiggle room. I had no boo, the last relationship I had ended in August 2019 and it ended badly. Almost throwing my purpose, my new life, and all my progress away; I decided to give God a year. I committed to no dating or talking to anyone for a year so I could realign myself with God and allow Him to heal my broken heart.

Between the no money and no boo, I had no plans! So, I decided to work instead of just sitting at home. Why waste a vacation day, right? In my prayer time that morning, I decided that I was going to have a good day. That I would see God's goodness, and I said my usual but sincere prayer to live in awe, wonder, and (reverential) fear of Him. I said, "God, I expect You to show up today for my birthday. I'm your daughter and You are a good Father." And off to work I went!

8:46am – Free Starbucks
8:50am – Paypal from Dad
10:08am – Free Redbox movie
10:30am – Customer interaction that resulted in one of my biggest sales this year (to date).
11:00am – Business referral
12:00pm – Cake and card from my coworkers
1:00pm – Free lunch from my coworker that had been at odds with me for the last three months.
1:40pm – New manager gives me a Dunkin Donuts gift card
11:19pm – Amazon gift card from a church friend (it was enough to buy both the planner and dream interpretation book I really wanted).
11:44pm – My small group coordinator sent me a message – a prayer over my purpose and life.

Let me tell you something. GOD SHOWED OUT!! I wanted to treat myself and I really couldn't afford it. Not even my favorite sushi for $13.00. Aspiring to be a better financial steward, I would not spend what I didn't have. And God made sure everything that day was paid for and special. It was literally a day of no stress. I went home, had a great dinner with my son, and watched a movie.

This did not even include all the wonderful affirming message that family and friends sent me. Affirmations of my worth, of my growth, of purpose… It was so much! A day that I would have remembered miserably is one of the most favorite ones I had this year. I went to sleep knowing my Father loves me and really sees me… I went to sleep full of joy.

> *The blessing of the LORD makes one rich, and He adds no sorrow with it.* – Matthew 10:22 NKJV

This is just one example of how amazing our Father is. If you really look and really think about it; I would guarantee that you will find God is highly active in your life. The moments you wanted coffee and had no money. When you feel alone and randomly someone sends you a loving message. When you are looking for an item in the store and it's sold out, but you find one misplaced further down in the aisle.

Dear Daughter of God, I want to encourage you to look forward to each day with expectation. And tell God that! I wake up every morning and, in my prayers, I express the desire to see God in my day - however He wants to show up. And the more He answers, the more my love and joy grows because this is not a one-way relationship, both parties are truly invested!

Prayer

Father God,

I thank you for being Jehovah Immeka – the Lord is with me. Help me to see the love notes you leave for me every day. The big and the small. I pray that as I begin to see You more, our relationship will grow deeper and strong. Help me to live a life full of gratitude, knowing that You choose to give freely, it is not by my merit. May I live every day in the wonder, awe, and fear of you (Proverbs 31:30 TPT).

In Jesus' name,
Amen

Love Moment

At the end of each day, review and/or document how God showed up. You should be able to always have at least 1 way that He showed His love for you. This is not the churchy cliché of "He protected me, He woke me up this morning and started me on my way." While those things are great, God deals with us personally. The more you reflect and look for Him, you'll find your list becomes longer.

Writing the love notes down is also good because in tough seasons, it reminds you of God's faithfulness. You have a personal resume with God, even if you can't see what He is doing currently

_____
_____
_____
_____
_____
_____
_____
_____
_____
_____
_____
_____
_____
_____
_____
_____

Like a flower in bloom,
I sit before my Father and allow
Him to make me over...
In His image.
With peace and love, He breathes
life in me.
With mercy and grace, He clothes
me.
With identity, He raises my head.
And with authority, He crowns me.
Never again will society define me,
Because the King of Glory claims
me.
His love for me, never a fleeting
thing.
It is the cornerstone to my very
being.

His Word is the garment of praise
turned wedding dress as I wait at
the door for Him.
Waiting to be presented, no longer
a princess but a Queen who's
patient.
Patient enough to wait for her
Father to set the stage and prepare
the tables...
The ones she once begged for
scraps at,
Didn't know how to act because she
was lost
But He restored her.
No longer wrapped in bandages but
heavenly linens highlighting her
purity.

This is destiny...
Where Father and daughter take
the first dance.
It is He who gets the first glance of
His craftsmanship before He
presents her to the world.
Just the greatest Father and His
girl.
And I'm proud of it.
His love - never failing and
completely mine.
And I, completely His.
What a peace, when heaven
touches earth,
With every forehead kiss, I smile.
Bowing low to His sovereignty,

He crowns me.
With His Spirit and Word, He
equips me.
I step forward to claim my
territory,
The Queen Standard rising.

- Crystal Antoinette Johnson

CPSIA information can be obtained
at www.ICGtesting.com
Printed in the USA
BVHW080743070521
606655BV00001B/316